On

The

Novice

Empire

An Essay

By Laymon Flack

"The Givers of Light are set in darkness and their children are placed amongst men."

On the Novice Empire

An Essay

By: Laymon Flack

Table of Contents

The Progression

Introduction   page 7

Section I   page 9

Section II   page 17

Section III   page 27

Section IV   page 55

Section V   page 89

Section VI   page 97

Section VII   page 113

Works Cited   page 123

Contact Info   page 125

Introduction

This is a perspicacious polemical work in response to that which has wrought so much, if not all of humanity's ills, the novice empire. Written in a succinct manner, the purpose of this essay is to philosophically explore the three main aspects of an empire. The human aspect, the economic aspect and the aspect of law are examined in a critical overview in hopes of allowing the reader to better understand why all empires have been novice at best, and how this affects us today. Further, the empires discussed in the succeeding pages are not just physical, but metaphysical as well. Both are integral to the development of humanity and it would be a disservice to the reader to discuss one without the other. With that being stated, there are those who learn for learning's sake and there are those who are educated as a means to an end. *The rail steers the train.*

I

"And what country can preserve its liberties, if its rulers are not warned from time to time, that this people preserve the spirit of resistance...The remedy is to set them right as to the facts."
Excerpt from a letter to William S. Smith from Thomas Jefferson

Like all novice empires before it, America has become a dependent nation. No longer able to conquer uncharted perceived indigenous territories rich in natural resources, it has, as with all global superpowers, resorted to a perpetual state of conflict abroad and domestic in order to mimic the wealth generated by the novice empires of old. Who, without outside provocation, in all cases, left a state of relative peace in their own countries to unjustly conquer their way back to a mirage of peace instead of being stuck in the state of constant warring America now finds itself. Our political system is democratic and our financial system is one that is capitalist in its now Darwinian form. For many years the arranged marriage of these two seemingly opposite systems worked for the free American and their loyal allies. Sadly, it is time for some long overdue counseling or worse, an amicable separation.

The problems arising from this marriage of institutions do not stem from the institutions themselves, but from the collective minds of maniacal men running these institutions. It is of the utmost importance at this point to mention that the seeds of a novice empire's destruction are sown at its inception. With that being said, let us begin.

The United States of America was founded by succeeding generations of those who fled England for the reason of religious persecution. Further, these same diaspora-esque people felt the tax imposed upon them by the King of England was unjust and this led to the want of independence from their monarchal homeland. In short, these people sought to physically distance themselves and when this would not suffice they sought to sever their obligatory financial ties from England, replacing the visible crown with a more furtive one. So what we find here is a group of people who felt they were religiously and financially treated unjustly and not seen as equals to their homeland constituents. Who ultimately sought, fought, and then gained their independence. We must now question

10

why this independence was so desperately wanted. It is not enough to be content merely with the aforementioned reasons. We must gain an understanding of what was being transferred to this new born nation.

First, like Rome before us, we replaced a King with a military leader and ascribed to him the less threating title of President in a similar way the Romans used Consul. As far as the people transitioning from one form of rule to the next, Niccolo Machiavelli wrote, "The same thing happens to a people which has been accustomed to live under foreign rulers...it forthwith returns to the yoke, and ofttimes to a heavier one than that which, a while back, it threw off its neck." This heavier yoke that the early Americans traded for began as a blade of grass upon their necks, but would eventually turn into the heavy rusting brass that we are so proudly burdened down with, through ignorance and a lack of knowledge.

Our forefathers also established a checks and balances system, consisting of three branches of government which are the judicial, legislative, and executive branches. This was meant to prevent our government from abusing its power by way of oppressing its citizens and served as the next evolutionary step in politics, born from the necessity of lessons learned from past monarchs. A similar idea was implemented in 1297 some four hundred plus years earlier in England with Parliament and the Magna Carta, a document which President Franklin Roosevelt felt held "democratic aspirations". Yet it was under English rule that America was called to be birthed, it was also under English rule that religious tolerance was not practiced and still, those democratic aspirations have not been achieved.

Following the Magna Carta in 1689 was the English Bill of Rights. Of this particular document for governing, Thomas Payne wrote, "if we will suffer ourselves to examine the component parts of the English constitution, we shall find them to be the base remains of two ancient tyrannies, compounded with some new republican materials." Payne went on to explain that the English constitution had remnants of not only monarchal, but aristocratic tyranny as well. He finally extrapolated that "To say that the constitution of England is a union of three powers reciprocally *checking* each other, is farcical." It is here where Thomas Payne misses the mark. From a concentration of power held solely by a king, then to have it split between king and parliament, to finally in America, where the idea of three separate but equal branches of government held this power is what is truly "farcical". The power of one, to the power of two, then to the power of three is the historical progression.

In all three of the aforementioned scenarios, the power is not in the hands of the people, it is still concentrated, wielded by the few elected officials, not by the one sovereign, as was seen with monarchies. So why would slightly skewed versions of the same style of governing work with a different set of people or the descendants of said people? It was not meant to work. It was merely a forced transference of power from the English king to the American president, from English parliament to the American government. The American Revolution was not a revolution at all, but a grab for power by men who simply wanted to rule, presented under the guise that everyone was fighting for independence. Fighting to break that heavy yoke that took the form of religious oppression placed upon the necks of those first settlers who acted out the seeking of freedom and independence. What they really sought was the freedom and independence to do the same which was done to them. To an extent, albeit a short extent, there was truth that the American Revolution was a fight for independence. However, the fight for independence was fought by soldiers, whereas the fight for power, the forerunner to absolute power, was fought with the pen by men who speculated on the future. What these men of speculation knew, or better worded, thought they discovered, was that by giving people the illusion their voice meant something in the political arena guaranteed a longer shelf life for the desired political system they so desperately sought to implement.

Only in extreme circumstances do political systems have long lives. Chinese Emperors and their dynastic rule were such a circumstance. Beginning close to four thousand years ago around 2100 BCE and lasting until 1912 AD, the Chinese had a succession of over five hundred emperors spanning twenty two dynasties over the course of thirty nine hundred years. A constant throughout the dynasties up until the Qing was the building, rebuilding, addition, and fortification of walls that stood along China's borders. This collection of walls would become what is known as the Great Wall of China, which was completed under the Ming Dynasty.

Though not the first of the dynasties, the Qin, which began in 221 BCE unified China by way of conquest and held power only a mere fifteen years through harsh rule and the suppression of any dissident thought. It was during the immediate preceding Zhou dynasty that Confucius lived and it would be in the succeeding Han dynasty that his philosophy would be first implemented and assimilated within the law. From Confucianism the idea of imperial examinations came[1]. These examinations allowed for the most qualified persons to hold official offices without bias, but solely based on their intelligence for the position. China, under the Song dynasty saw the power of the Emperor go from being absolute[2] to semi-checked, in part due to the imperial examinations placing high level thinkers in official positions who argued well the importance of following Confucian[3] thought. So at least twenty years before the writing of the Magna Carta we see Chinese politics siphoning power from their ruler and placing it in the hands of their few examine proven officials.

---

[1] The modern civil service exams can trace some of their origins to these imperial examinations.

[2] This idea of absolute power was held the same by English Kings who felt their rule was by divine right, but was also lessened with the creation of the Magna Carta during King Edward's reign.

[3] An interesting side note is that the first known use of the English word confusion (meaning misperception or error of interpretation, mental disorientation) was in 14th century Europe. A slight deviation from the word Confucian.

It is worthwhile to note that China would allow one man's, Confucius, philosophical thought, to wield so much influence over public policy. In this sense, through death, Confucius becomes the ghost of Plato's Philosopher King, influencing the policies of a Chinese Kallipolis. Correctly called so because in life he "genuinely and adequately philosophized" and in death his philosophy was semi-implemented throughout an entire empire, leaving every Chinese Emperor who applied it, an unwitting loyal subject.

II

Capitalism is the means by which the world's economy i.e. the free market operates and exists in modern society. America is the breeding ground for young capitalist in grooming, so much so, that our nation's capital is not a state nor a commonwealth, but a lone district set apart by itself allowing no one state to claim the capital as its own. The Unanimous Declaration of the Thirteen United States of America tells us that we have certain unalienable rights bestowed upon us by our creator[4]. Among those rights are liberty, the pursuit of happiness, and life. It is understood that liberty is, "the absence of externall Impediments: which Impediments, may oft take away part of a mans power to do what hee would."

This is the argument used by those who detest big government and favor unregulated private business. At the heart of this argument is the liberty to do what one wants. It is a law of nature that, "a man is forbidden to do that, which is destructive of his life,

---

[4] It is important to note that it is a written document that informs a person of the rights giving to them by the one who created human beings. For those who scoff at the idea of a creator, then of those rights issued by the equitable circumstances which brought all things into being on Earth.

or taketh away the means of preserving the same; and to omit, that, by which he thinketh it may be preserved." In a time when corporations are freely giving the "unalienable rights" of life, liberty, and the pursuit of happiness under the auspicious title of "Corporate Personhood" without the responsibility of being an actual person/human, is not the only true unalienable right left for actual human beings the pursuit, and only the pursuit of happiness? Yet while achieving happiness through the pursuit guaranteed ultimately harms those in this very same pursuit.

This is so because the design of the system in which the pursuit is guaranteed is limited in size and scope, hence the irrational need to spread democracy and capitalism throughout the world, so as to enlarge the system so more can achieve this now contrived democratic Darwinian capitalist happiness. Or so we are meant to think or in fact it may be truth, time will have to reveal this. Now a corporation's officers have a fiduciary duty to pursue and maintain profits for shareholders and cannot on purpose avoid pursuing profits, as this would put the corporation at odds with state laws. Is this not in accordance with one of the laws of nature? In fact, there is nothing neither wrong nor evil with a corporation. It is not wrong for a corporation to be granted this "Corporate Personhood" title either. The wrong lies with the people who mismanage them.

In theory, a corporation has the ability to accomplish, by way of its copious amount of finances and vast influence, great feats of ingenuity which countless people with the mental acumen cannot, simply because they lack the level of finances and technology needed. It is not that the corporation is used, rather it is misused. Corporations are not managed they are mismanaged and misused by the very same people who cry out for smaller government, the privatization of many of the public services the government provides. For what purpose is this cry if not to transfer power from one leviathan to another? Not for an over-abundance of fear is this done, no, for the want of profit, that yearn for power, the misnomer that the rest of the world views in America, but these types of American's would rather gouge their eyes out than take notice of.

Even the corporations and those wealthy few who practice false philanthropy, examples being, giving money for research into the dying off of honey bees, studies about the effects of poverty on a child's educational development, to the building of state of the art educational facilities at Ivy league schools, anything but giving directly to those who are oppressed under a capitalist system where their "pursuit of happiness" is in slow progress or has stalled out for one reason or another, albeit their own fault or the fault of someone else. Who then can hold these wealthy few culpable for surrounding the problem with finances in futile hopes of finding solutions instead of admitting that the solution is within the problem and dealing with it directly? For by being philanthropic to those whose pursuit is still in progress they are giving away that which gives them a significant percent of their power to the very same people who would quite possibly do the same as them giving the right circumstances.

In his song "Guns and Roses", Jay-z raps, "They say when you play with skills good luck will happen." Renowned artist Henry Hartman even said, "Success always comes when preparation meets opportunity." How hard is it then to hit this non-equestrian trifecta to achieve the pursuit of happiness, to have those right circumstances giving when in a capitalist society a thing must be taking? The corporation does not share the same unalienable rights with human beings. The only unalienable right a corporation has is, "the pursuit of equitable profits"[5]. Meaning equitable financial profits and

---

[5] If we are to give rights to entities we give life to, corporations or whatever

equitable profits which advance the human race, as the corporation was birthed from the human race for the advancement of the human race no matter if this is openly admitted or not. The "pursuit of equitable profits" is the closest equivalency to our pursuit of happiness that the corporation shall have.

Now those who desperately cry out for smaller government, deregulation, and the privatization of many if not all things, cry out for not only their own oppression, but the oppression of the whole of society. The point of three separate but equal branches of government was for the checks and balance of each other, to deter widespread corruption and to prevent one person from wielding absolute power over a whole society. The crown was, has, and always will be privatized. This is one of the unspoken reasons why monarchs always faced the threat of regicide. A king is king by divine right[6], this dates further back than Hammurabi and even was seen with the English crown, even more still, it is biblical. When

---

future endeavors hold, they need be rights that benefit humans, not supersede our own rights to our detriment. For when this occurs the entity does harm to humans, in this case the corporation does harm to humans in the name of un-equitable financial profit. An example of this is the Supreme Court case Kiobel v Royal Dutch Petroleum.

[6] This idea of divine right will be discussed in section IV

Saul[7], from the tribe of Benjamin was chosen by the people to be

their king they chanted, "God save the King!"[8] When David took

the royal city of the children of Am'mon he placed their defeated

king's crown on his head and it weighed a talent of gold, somewhere

around seventy-five pounds[9]. Both of these Kings' counsel was God

who also was the source of their divinity, a figure to some[10] that is

nonexistent, which would mean that they took up counsel unto

themselves. In other words, privatizing the crown, a practice that

remained until the monarchal society outgrew the crown and treated

their non-philosopher kings to regicide or outwitted them politically.

　　If those who seek to have major highways privatized, have

the health care system privatized, and remanded to the private sector

to do with what they like, whom or what would keep these industries

checked and balanced? Shall the lives of countless millions be

---

[7] Saul was chosen because of his height and good looks to be king. Also the tribe of Benjamin was the tribe who raped a woman, forcing her husband to divided her body into twelve parts, sending them to the other tribes to show the lewdness of their act believing he was dead, an offence that they paid dearly for. It is of no coincidence then that King Saul was who he was. Judges 19 & 20

[8] 1 Samuel 10:24

[9] 2 Samuel 12:30

[10] To those who choose not to believe in God or the idea of divinity through him, then divine right defined as, "the monarchal rule accomplished through absolute belief in one's own purpose then transposing this belief onto others until the whole or at least a majority of society believes the same", should suffice.

decided by a corporation whose sole purpose is to generate profits? Shall fellow corporations check and balance fellow corporations to the detriment of the "Corporate Race?" Is not a man "forbidden to do that, which is destructive of his life, or taketh away the means of preserving the same?" If privatization occurs on the scale which these maniacal people would have it and the responsibility of government shrinks, then the odds of corruption and biased policy making will also increase exponentially. Not to say that corruption and biased policy making does not occur at present, but without a set of people who have minimum (the system in place now) to no stake (what we hope to achieve) in the private sector, then this will become law. That is to say, be accepted. At worse accept as law by those whom this practice will harm the most.

Both government and the private sector need votes to put people in official positions. However, the difference lies in how the people qualify to be eligible voters. The difference is simple, to vote in the private sector you have to buy your way in, simply stated, be a shareholder. To vote in governmental elections you have to be at least eighteen years of age and a legal citizen. What then happens to the non-shareholder when the private sector, the realm of the corporate race, size increases to the point it surpasses the size of a shrinking government?

A transition occurs, much the same way the crown became just a figurehead to remind the English people of what they had when parliament along with the Prime Minister began sharing the crown's lost power. The president becomes the figure head and the corporate board room replaces the three branches of government. Those who cannot buy their way in will have no vote, meaning they will have no say in who makes the decisions in the country they reside. How then can a people survive being a "citizen inmate" walking with perceived freedom in one's own country? Laws are no longer constitutional they become a set of corporate bylaws regulating a Correctional Facility Nation where the richest inmates are divided from the middle and lower class, willingly imprisoning themselves behind gates for convenience. Or is it they who imprison the middle and lower class? Doing so by first economically separating them-self and then by physically having gates punctuate the separation.

Like the Chinese emperors who built, rebuilt, and added to the Great Wall to protect their citizens from invaders and preserve social order, so does the corporate race do for its richest inmates, building, rebuilding, and adding economic walls[11] along with physical gates, until the nation is figuratively and literally divided amongst itself. To what purpose is this done? To whose advantage is this for? Again, it is not the corporation that is wrong or evil, it is the maniacal people who mismanage and misuse these corporations for their own selfish end, siphoning this gained power to the few while using it to oppress the misinformed masses.

---

[11] A reference to Wendy Brown's essay "Walled States, Waning Sovereignty" where she discusses the idea of walls separating certain aspects of society.

III

How can a people obey or follow a set of laws they know little to nothing about? For that matter, why are the laws of America, the United States Codes (USC), not taught at the earliest age possible like reading, science, arithmetic, writing, history, and language so as to make sure that every citizen knows what is acceptable and what is not acceptable behavior? Let us define code before continuing. A code is a puzzle, cipher, or a thing that a person lives by. The latter is not applicable to the USC and will be shown why later in this section.

Thomas Hobbes wrote, "Law made, if not also made known, is no law." So how then shall law be made if not openly by the elected officials a nation of people vote into office? On this subject Jean-Jacques Rousseau then wrote, "But when the people as a whole makes rules for the people as a whole, it is dealing with itself…without any division whatever…And *this* is the kind of act which I call a law." It is here that we will, with purpose, deviate slightly from the topic of law and make mention that only two things give out time[12]. One is the creation of life, the other, our justice system. What then does this say about the justice system, better yet what does this say about where we place that judicial branch under which it falls and the power that we give to it?

Four major penalties exist in response to breaking the law. They are, ordered in the severity of the crime they allude to remedy, probation, a fine, being sentence to time (either by performing communal service or inside of some prison), or death. Now those who study and learn the law are more apt to avoid punishment. We cannot say avoid punishment for breaking the law, as the USC has many a loophole by which those with the time and finances can navigate safely through undetected while those who do not, suffer the consequences[13]. Worse still, not just the laymen, but even our higher educated citizens have little to no idea how to phrase, let alone ask the right questions in respect to law.

---

[12] We will discuss this dichotomy of time held d by the justice system in section IV.

[13] In 2010 General Electric, a corporation, grossed a profit of over four billion dollars while their federal income tax rate was a dismal -76.6%, meaning they paid no tax on their earned income. In this same year they received "$3.3 billion in net tax benefits from the United States government." Conversely, also in 2010, actor Wesley Snipes, a human being, was imprisoned for three years on a 2008 conviction for failing to pay $12 million dollars in taxes on income he earned from 1999-2001. We must note that it was a willful failure to pay his taxes.

If you were to ask a law enforcement officer, a judge, or even a lawyer, how many laws there were governing the citizens of the United States of America[14], you would be hard-pressed to receive a definitive number. Their answers, though not numeric would go along these lines, "Well, you cannot give them a specific number because there are federal laws, state laws, local laws, military laws, tort laws." No doubt each answer would be some variation of these preceding words. Then if the exact number of laws is not known it can be deduced that the specific content of each law is not known either. If the specific content of each law is not known, then how can law be properly followed or enforced? Let alone how can new laws then be passed when the existing ones are not adequately known by all who fall under their jurisdiction enforce, interpret, or practice them? So now let us look at the law enforcement officer, the judge, and the lawyer for they represent three separate aspects of law. One is for the enforcement of law, the other is for the interpretation of the law, and the latter is for the practice of the law.

---

[14] Even this question can be considered phrased wrong or is the wrong question in general for the solicitation of the proper answer we are looking for.

Let us begin with the lawyer, the legal practitioner of law. We say legal practitioner of law for whenever a person who is not a lawyer decides to represent themselves as was the case with Colin Ferguson[15], or any of the extremist groups who proclaim they need not a license to drive, nor pay taxes to the government; the public deems these as the "insightful ramblings of madmen."[16] Also, more times than not these persons are found guilty. It is the lawyer's duty to argue for the defendant while it is the job of the prosecutor to, well, to prosecute the defendant. It is understood in the court of law that the defendant is, "presumed innocent until proven guilty", a statement which is contradictory by way of the treatment and label, "defendant", placed upon the person in question, who has been "accused", we will now dissect.

The defendant is accused not because they are presumed innocent, but they are accused because someone presumed that they are guilty of a crime. From this presumption they are removed from

---

[15] The man who in 1993 shot twenty-five people, killing six of them on the Long Island Rail Road then decided to defend himself in what was viewed as one of the most bizarre cases in recent New York history.

[16] This phrase only points out how the common citizen rarely gets to see how a deemed "lunatic" thinks and when they do they are usually appalled to see how the deemed "lunatic" views themselves as the victim when it is the deemed "lunatic" who did the actual victimizing. Thus the common citizen has a perceived better insight of lunacy.

their regular day to day activities and placed into the custody of the justice system, where, if deemed fit, a sum of money, known as bail, is set, and if met, lets this person have restrictive freedom on the promise that they will obey the guidelines set forth by a judge at their bail hearing. With restrictive freedom comes the fact they have lost a portion of their unalienable rights, liberty, "the absence of externall Impediments: which...may oft take away part of a mans power to do what hee would." Why then would a person lose any of their unalienable rights except for life, as all people must at some point, unless they were guilty of a crime or at least accused of a crime, meaning they are presumably guilty? A person does not lose their unalienable rights for being accused of innocence, no. It can then be surmised that the defendant is, "presumed guilty until proven innocent", as the system takes away their freedom and to regain a temporary semblance of this freedom, the defendant must pay the system that attempts to prosecute them.

Now, even though there are two supposed equal opposing sides in a trial with a judge presiding over the courtroom, it is not an equal playing field. This is best illustrated by the fact that no sane person ever freely walks into a court room on their own accord, not being charged with a crime, unaware of any crime, proclaiming innocence in general then asks to be put on trial for any crime the court sees fit, based on the fact that innocence or guilt is determined on the better argument. Evidence and testimony included in the idea of the argument. Further, jurors are told of what the defendant is accused of, but in the contradictory manner that has become the norm in the justice system, the jurors are then told to not judge the defendant on what he/she is accused of, but to solely go on the facts, the evidence presented during the trial and only during trial. It is here where the intelligence of the justice system and the intelligence the justice system credit the jurors with having come into question.

How can an intelligent person be told the "defendant" is "accused" of, let's say murder, and not question why this person is even being "accused" in the first place? For if a person is truly innocent why would they be in this current predicament to begin with? Herein lies the fundamental flaw with the statement "presumed innocent until proven guilty", it is meant to give the illusion of something that is not truly there, the same way that those men of speculation knew what giving the illusion of an equal voice meant to their ideology's longevity. In this case the fundamental flaw is the illusion of a fair and balanced trial.

Concerning the argument that the lawyer and prosecutor partake in to win their case, the argument becomes a cruel and unusual form of temporary reality for the person who is no longer a person but a defendant who stands accused. This cruel and unusual state between innocence and guilt is likened to the biblical verse where Jesus spoke saying, "I know thy works, that thou art neither cold nor hot: I would thou wert cold or hot. So then because thou art lukewarm, and neither cold nor hot, I will spue thee out of my mouth."[17] When a person is accused and doubt is raised to whether they are innocent or guilty friends, neighbors, even family will sometimes abandon them, i.e. spue thee out, until the accusations are cleared up. And all of this is determined by an argument where reasonable doubt has to be raised in order to exonerate the person who has become a "defendant" standing "accused", uprooted from their regular day to day activities on the words of another[18].

---

[17] Revelation 3:16

[18] This is not always the case, for some people are actually red-handedly guilty and a trial would be just a formality. However, since the outcome is based on how well either side argues, a trial can never truly be a formality unless the jurors have been bought or have a preconceived idea of their verdict, in which case they

Now the argument is presented with evidence and witnesses to strengthen each respective side of the case. A person that is flawed can always serve justice, but a system and process that is flawed cannot, much the same way a cogwheel with one triangle tipped tooth when in motion if the rest of the teeth have flattened edges will harm the whole of the machine. How then is this justice when a person can accuse another of being guilty of a crime and that person has to go to trial or at least be questioned on account of the accusation, but a person cannot walk out of a court room a free man if another person walks in during a trial and accuses the same of being innocent?

To make this matter worse, individuals have different levels of intelligence. So the lawyer may be less intelligent than the prosecutor and vice versa. Add to the fact that some people are better at articulating themselves than others and this rabbit hole gets deeper. Keep in mind that this is happening to a person, who is accused, presumed innocent until proven guilty, who now is subjected to factors beyond his or her control that will ultimately

---

have negated the instructions of only going on the evidence presented at the trial and only during the trial, flawing the system of justice even further.

decide their fate in the court of law simply on the word of another. Let us not forget the intelligence of the person who stands accused, for it is they who must decide on their lawyer, and if they can afford a good lawyer. Let us hope they can decide on an intelligent, honest, truth seeking lawyer who must defend them against a system who collects taxes not only from the said accused, but from the peers of the said accused, and some of these taxes are allocated to pay the very same prosecutor, who, in a twisted case of irony attempts to prosecute the accused, whose tax dollars actually help pays their salary. Seeing as though most people do not collect taxes from their peers and allocate some of these taxes for a division of well-trained highly educated lawyers, who then has the upper-hand in the courtroom?

It is now true that justice is blind. It is blind to the truth and depends on persons who have monetary gains at stake i.e. lawyers, prosecutors, and judges as its seeing-eye dogs to lead to the truth. That is why at the end of trials the prosecutor and lawyer so often shake hands in a sportsmanlike manner, because they are the athletes in the courtroom while the accused defendant is the tennis ball mercilessly volleyed back and forth between innocence and guilt via the argument until the match is over. This is also why after being found guilty, whether the verdict of guilt is truth or not, the defendant can have people speak on their behalf and beg the court for leniency. Make no error in thought. A game is being played with people's lives here.

To conclude this matter on the absurdity of the argument and of the lawyer, we must return our gaze back to Colin Ferguson. It is because a system is in place where arguments decide the fate of a person that he was allowed to make not only a mockery of the people he injured and murdered, but also of the courts. With video evidence, countless witnesses, his fingerprints on the weapons, this man was still allowed to defend himself against what, if not his own guilt. He was not sentenced to death instead he received three hundred fifteen years and eight months in prison. His imprisonment will cost taxpayers somewhere around forty-plus thousand dollars a year. He murdered six people, some who had decent paying jobs, but now his imprisonment has cost taxpayers more than the people he murdered were putting into the system. Yes, this raises many ethical, moral, and societal financial questions on many different levels.

We will now discuss the interpreter of law, the judge. A lawgiver, as described by Rousseau deals with a dilemma of sorts, a contradiction, "a task which is beyond human powers and a non-existent authority for its execution." Though not a lawgiver, a judge deals with a similar dilemma, to pass a sentence on a person based on the verdict giving by twelve of the accused peers, when, in some cases his opinion on the same set of evidence differs. And to seek the proper sentencing from a "non-existent authority" is the flipside to this. In either case what is the virtue of this judge, what direction does his/her moral compass point and what or who is the "non-existent authority" from which the judge determines sentencing?

A sentencing table from the Federal Sentencing Guideline Manual is what is used by the judge to determine the required sentencing. This sentencing table consists of a vertical column numbered from one to forty-three and this is for the offense level of the crime. There is also a horizontal row labeled in roman numerals one to six for the criminal history category, where criminal points are added up. Where the cross section of these rows and columns meet determines the sentencing. So for example, any offense level from thirty-seven up with a criminal history category of six can get

37

the perceived guilty person life. The further up the offense level goes the lower the level of criminal history has to be in order to get life, so by offense level forty-three, a category one criminal history will get the defendant life.

Now the only way guidelines can be set is by the establishing of a pattern(s) of criminal behavior, law breaking, by which the patterns are then measured and categorized, formulating these guidelines. These patterns are measured after the person's first arrest and conviction when they are initially put into the penal system, a subsystem of the justice system, by the amount of times the person is in court or by the amount of times they are incarcerated and what they are incarcerated for. From this, the individual human being is of no more concern, only the sentencing guidelines that have been established from the gathered data from these patterns of behavior produced over time throughout the United States by human beings. Since no one is born anything into this world except for their gender, and are molded by those around them and the environments they inhabit throughout life, no one is born a criminal. Yet little to none of this is taking into account at federal sentencing by the judge except what the federal guidelines say.

Even worse, outside of kidnapping, murder, and rape[19] all of the punishable crimes listed under the federal guidelines deal with some kind of monetary value. From tax evasion to the illegal sales of fire arms, narcotics, terrorism, copyright infringement, etc. the loss of monetary gain is involved. What is truly sad about the terrorism part of the guidelines is that throughout the nineteenth and twentieth century, African-Americans suffered under the Ku Klux Klan acts of domestic terrorism that were appalling, Black Wall Street[20] is just one horrendous example. The reason these acts went unpunished was the ties that the KKK held to politicians. Politicians who passed laws, in some cases criminal laws that judges then would use federal guidelines to determine how to sentence the offenders of these laws. The offenders of these laws convicted were mostly the spoken minority, not the actual minority.

The point of mentioning all of this is that one such tie was Strom Thurmond. Not to say he actual had physical connections to

---

[19] Rape being defined as the sexual violation of one's person against their will; Extortion being omitted because it is a crime that includes some kind of monetary gain which eliminates it from a natural crime

[20] A prosperous black community existing during the early 20th century in the Greenwood section of Tulsa Oklahoma that was torched on the words of someone that a black boy had assaulted a white girl

this nefarious terrorist group, but the tie lied in the same segregationist ideology they shared. In 1958 Senator Strom Thurmond held the longest filibuster by a single senator lasting over twenty-four hours, all in the hopes of preventing the Civil Rights Act from being passed. An act that would help towards the fruition of the idea that all people are created equal and deserve to be treated as such was what the Senator was against. Going back further to 1948 in his campaign speech Strom Thurmond spoke these words, "I wanna tell you, ladies and gentlemen, that there's not enough troops in the army to force the Southern people to break down segregation and admit the Negro race into our theaters, into our swimming pools, into our homes[21], and into our churches." It is not that his words can be interpreted as racist it is the fact that the senator put states' rights above human rights. He put the liberty of the state over the liberty of another human being simply because of the color of their skin. Keep in mind that a state, the interior of a set of boundaries separating naturally connected pieces of land, in most cases the whole land, is yet another creation of human beings. This was done in the name of

---

[21] Years prior to giving this speech a 22 year old Strom Thurmond would end up impregnating his family's 16 year African-American maid who oddly enough cleaned the inside of his parents' home.

"preserving a more perfect union", which is to say the system is of higher value than the very same thing that created it viz. the created is greater than the creator.

Strom Thurmond served as a United States senator from 1954 until 2001, helping to pass laws that his fellow Americans would have to adhere to. The sum of his words and actions was an inference that all men are not created equal. How then can a man who believes in segregation be allowed to help create and pass laws that the whole of society had to obey when he felt that society should not be integrated? This could only be possible if the senator had been rehabilitated of his wayward views and actions in regards to his ability to without prejudice create and pass laws. The act of his filibuster helped perpetuate the violence against the Negro in America, making him what some would consider, even the Federal Sentencing Guidelines Manual would describe as, an accessory.

So if the senator could be rehabilitated then why not convicted persons after they are released from prison? The government labels these people as ex-convicts, in some cases they are never allowed to vote in public elections again, jobs take into consideration if a person has been convicted of a crime and depending on the crime will hold it against them. In effect these people are labeled with a malicious tag for the rest of their lives, outliers to the society they were born in over a lapse or perceived lapse of judgment during a particular moment in their lives. Yet a self-professed segregationist was allowed to help create and pass laws for close to fifty years over an entire nation simply because he kept being voted in by people who we dared not called racist or segregationist at the turn of the new millennium.

The Volstead Act of 1919 prohibited the manufacturing, sale, distribution, and consumption of alcohol. This act was repealed fourteen years later in 1933, but what was done was done already. In Philadelphia alone the arrest per year went from "75,618 in 1919 to 137,263 in 1925" and this could be attributed to the new act that banned alcohol.

Now the reason for this long diatribe about everything but judges is to show some of information that they are or at least should be equipped with. They know the statistics on prohibition, yet they still, at the supreme level allow for substances to be banned. If this allowance is not for some monetary gain for the few then for what is its purpose? A substance that exists can only be made illegal to the detriment of the people from which it is prohibited[22]. The judge is aware of all the aforementioned information so every time he/she has to pass a sentence that judge has a choice to make. Either, continue punishing his/her fellow human being until the whole of society is completely broken in the name of preserving a flawed system or break the system in the name of advancing his/her fellow flawed human beings. The judge cannot make the choice because the judge is only concerned with the now, the present moment, their present purpose. The trial at hand and only the trial at hand is their concern, tied to the same orders giving to the juror. In this way they are forever present in the said trial, confined to the guidelines provided by the justice system of which they too are a part of. Like the corporation, again we see a thing giving life to by human beings that ultimately begins to wield power over the human being.

We have looked at and examined the lawyer and the judge, now we will turn and view the enforcer of the law, the law enforcement officer the physical extension of the law. It is the

---

[22] Policing a person's body leads to the policing of a person's mind which leaves the person no freedom because the person is already policed under societal law just so he/she can live in society. A life with no liberty or the allowance of the pursuit of happiness is evolved slavery in its beginning stage.

existence of the law enforcement officer that shows the fallibility of the law itself. For true law requires no enforcement because true law is inextricably connected to its adherence which is inextricably connected to order which is the foundation upon which all things civil should be built. The only time enforcement is required is when a people as a whole in society do not agree with such laws. Meaning the law is meant to protect those who created the law and those who align themselves with the creators of the law. At such a time, a divide is then formed and one side must enforce its will onto the other in the form of law in what they believe is the only way to preserve social order. This constitutes one of the many flaws in law. To prevent a thing such as this from happening Rousseau wrote that the decemvirs[23] of Rome said, "Nothing we propose to you…can become law without your consent. Romans, be yourselves the authors of the laws which are to ensure your happiness." It would only seem right then that a government, when they are about to create a new law should at least hold a general election for that law, the same way primaries and presidential elections are held. It is not

---

[23] A term in Latin meaning "ten men", these men were chosen to write a set of laws for the Republic of Rome.

farfetched to think that a people would take time out of their day to go vote on a new gun law much the same way they go out to vote for a new mayor or governor, but this is not the case.

So what we have is a system creating laws to impose its will, not in secret, but not exactly in the public eye either. By doing so the system empowers its extension, the law enforcement officer to further impose the system's will. As the size, degree, and scope of power the law enforcement officer is endowed with to exercises the will of the system that empowers them increases, the more that the happiness of the people decreases. Regardless of being in agreement or not with the law, the setting of perimeters around one's freedom by these laws will eventually lead to the demoralization by way of the ensuing claustrophobia suffered by one's will at this point unless the whole of society is on one accord with the whole sum these laws. For how can the pursuit of happiness and the guarantee of liberty be fully actualized when there are those enforcing a will of a system in the form of law over the whole of society when a portion of the populace quite possibly in their hearts and mind resists it?

To maintain the role of enforcement officer of the law, the officer has to now disavow themselves from their own beliefs and unequivocally take on the beliefs of the system which is the system's written law. By doing so, the officer is unaligned with the people he/she is sworn to protect and serve and is then aligned with the system. In other words, an officer cannot properly protect and serve those who do not agree with the proposed way they are to be protected and served. Here is where the saying, "you sometimes have to protect a person from themselves" comes into play. What then is the way that you can protect a person, or a whole of society from themselves without taking away the guarantee of liberty, life in the sense of how they live it, and the pursuit of happiness? The law has become in direct conflict with our nation's founding documents and the enforcers of such laws are at odds with its people whether they or the people acknowledge it or not.

The true insult to the idea of a law enforcement officer and an even greater insult to the people they are sworn to protect are the low standards required in order to pass police exams. In New York City the police officer's exam is meant, "to gauge the cognitive ability, observational skills, and mental acuity of interested applicants. These are the traits that have been determined to be important to the effective performance of your duties as an Officer."

The basic requirements are those of any person who is not at the very low end of the learning spectrum. It becomes no wonder that we so frequently are bombarded with news of law enforcement officers on administrative leave or suspension with pay following some absurd incident involving a plunger, multiple rounds fired into an unarmed citizen, or unwarranted stop and frisks. It is the process by which the officers are recruited that allows for the influx of the worst possible candidates and very few who are of exceptional intelligence. As long as a person is of low intelligence they are easily ordered and comply with no resistance. This is what the system needs in their officers, someone who does not ask questions in regards to the law, who follows orders and enforces the law, period. These are also the expectations held for the people who are subjected to the law and expected to obey it, total compliance.

If we were to look a level up at the FBI, the federal bureau of investigations, another law enforcement agency higher up than the police officer, we will see that the requirements are a bit more stringent. For one, a college degree is required, which should be the standard for all law enforcement officers. It is also at the federal level that they pursue the real intelligent "criminals"[24], while on the police level, either local or state they come across intelligent "criminals" every once in a while and when they do, the FBI is usually called in to help with the investigation. So even in law enforcement, the low intelligence chase the low intelligences and the high intelligence pursue the high intelligence. To conclude this matter, the law enforcement officer finds themselves in a conundrum because they want to serve the people the only way they feel they can, which is through law enforcement, but the system that produces these laws which these officers enforce are blinded by corruption due to the ever increasingly Darwinian capitalist society in which we live.

Now that we have looked at the enforcer of the law, the interpreter of the law, and the practitioner of the law let us conclude all matters on the subject of law in this section by looking at why law has failed us. The reason it has failed is due to corruption, or what is commonly referred to as "business" in a capitalist society. The corporation has permeated the justice system and since its only goal is to maintain profits, by its very nature it corrupts the system.

---

[24] The use of quotations around the word criminal is to signify that they are only criminal by law, a point that will be made later in this section, proven how this title has become null and void.

True justice cannot keep the company of monetary value for when it does, monetary value dictates law and the corporation determines what justice is. By now we know that justice for the corporation is profit.

An example of this corruption is the partnership between several agencies of local and Federal Government and the Correctional Corporation of America, commonly referred to as the CCA, a company publicly traded since 1994 on the NYSE under the symbol CXW. Immediately this terrible contradiction is apparent in the preceding sentence. According to CCA's website, it maintains, "its market leadership position in private corrections, managing more than 40 percent of all adult-secure beds under contract with such providers in the United States." It goes on to say that, "As a full-service corrections management provider, CCA specializes in the design, construction, expansion and management of prisons, jails and detention facilities, as well as inmate transportation services through its subsidiary company TransCor America." If the CCA builds these facilities and provides 40 percent of the United States correctional facilities beds, then United States has to have bodies placed into these facilities with beds or they will be losing copious amounts of money, fulfilling the adage "a business with no clients is a business with no money." Since neither the government nor the CCA are in the business of losing money, a way to provide bodies into these facilities has to be created. Even worse than the CCA is the GEO which is the world's largest provider of correctional facilities. Both corporations' partnership with each of their respective governments' raise the question as to if a corporation's responsibility is to create and maintain profits for its shareholders, "how do they propose to create and maintain these profits when the means by which this is achieved is through housing, transportation, and alleged rehabilitation of breakers of each governments' law?" With the asking of this question another more important one has to be asked which is "if a government has to create laws to govern its citizens and maintain social order, how then can they provide the necessary bodies needed to fill these correctional facilities that are being built by the corporations they are in a partnership with unless the reasoning behind creating laws has shifted?"

One of the key phrases in the CCA's mission statement is when it says that CCA "specializes" in "the expansion and management of…detention facilities as well as inmate transportation." This means the corporation expands its facilities at a sustainable cost by accepting a greater number of inmates. By the creation of new laws and the more stringent enforcement of older ones, the justice system is able to provide law enforcement agencies with the necessary tools to acquire what we will refer to as their "commodities", i.e. deemed criminals, for the CCA. So if the government is creating laws to insure that contract obligations are met for their corporate partners like CCA and GEO then the purpose of law has shifted from the maintaining of a civil society to maintaining a sustainable source of income for corporations.

To illustrate how this is truly condemning society without society even being aware, since 1994 CCA has been publicly traded. So for every citizen incarcerated after 1994 their conviction has to be seriously scrutinized because the laws made after this point have the chance of being influenced by the monetary gain of the CCA and corporations like it, hence the calling of the justice system corrupt. It is no longer justice, but the secondary stage of slavery developing again in its evolved form. Now that we have shown how the creation of law has become corrupt at its core due to the obligations government has to their corporate family member to provide them with "commodities", i.e. deemed criminals to be traded from one correctional facility to the next for monetary gain, we will briefly discuss the USC, as more words than we would have liked has been already used on this subject.

Earlier in this section we defined the word code as a "puzzle, cipher, or a thing that a person lives by." It is of the utmost importance that here we state, "Government is the parent of all corporations." With that being said it becomes easy to see why government and corporations coexist so easily, they are of the same corporate race. Corporations such as General Electric have a division of lawyers whose sole purpose is dedicated to handling their taxes. As demonstrated earlier in this section they not only avoid paying taxes, but the government gives them a hefty tax return though it is not labeled as such. The government for their part has a tax code, by some estimates it is anywhere between five thousand to eleven thousand pages in length. This style of code is perfectly suited for corporations to decipher, and at the same time poorly suited for the average citizen, who sees this as a terrifying jigsaw puzzle to begin to comprehend.

So it is the corporation who has the ability to thrive and exist under such a lengthy code constructed by government. Now human beings have created two entities that simultaneously wield power over them, one the offspring of the other, and quite possibly to our very detriment. Niccolo Machiavelli wrote, "and if it be a question of either of them loosed from control by the law, there will be found fewer errors in the populace than in the prince." Translated for the modern society, the populace is still the populace, but the government is now king and the corporation has become prince.

IV

"If we are to build a better world, we must have the courage to make a new start-even if that means some *reculer pour mieux sauter.*"

Socialization is not arbitrary in the sense that it is equally for humanity's progress nor is it equally for our destruction. Since humans have been living in communities, somewhere around forty thousand years, socialization has occurred. It can be argued that this process takes us away from purpose, while the same argument can be made that it brings forth purpose. Before continuing let us define socialization so as to do away with any confusion that may arise. Socialization is the act of learning from those around you while at the same time learning how to live with those around you and this is accomplished through the constant mingling and interaction with other people who are part of the whole of humanity ergo socialization. It is this constant struggle embedded in the definition of socialization that causes humanity so much of its woes while at the same time creating what seems at least for now great feats of human ingenuity. There is a familiar saying in the United States that goes, "It's not what you know it's who you know." Following in the same vein is this saying's fraternal twin which goes, "It's not what you know it's what you can prove."

The first of these sayings places a greater value on socialization than it does on intelligence. The second of these sayings places greater value on evidence over truth, no matter if it is truth or not as long as the evidence is viable, it becomes truth in the court of law. If both of these sayings hold true, as both seem to, especially with the advent of the internet age, then intelligence and truth are required to play fourth fiddle to socialization and to whatever is practical to be considered true at the time. With that being said, anyone who agrees with the aforementioned sayings cannot disagree with the statement, "Sociability is of greater importance to humanity than intelligence." They also cannot say in response, "but the two are of equal importance" or "the two are not mutually exclusive", because at this point they are speaking the flaw, visualizing the flaw, yet denying what they are speaking and visualizing is a flaw at all.

Once intelligence has been placed underfoot of socialization, all forms of chaos[25] from the mundane to the very extreme begin to occur. The obvious example is the simultaneously extreme prosperity and extreme suffering German people experienced under Adolf Hitler's Nazi regime from 1933-1945. In the aftermath of WWI with U.N. sanctions confining their military ambitions, along with justifiable financial payments Germany had to make under the Treaty of Versailles that further crippled their economy, intelligence was cast aside for chaos. Instead of looking at each one of themselves as individuals and providing a solution to their postwar situation, Germany's collective ear was poisoned by Hitler's serpentipis words. Chaos took shape in the form of renewed military ambition and a genocide allowing millions to be killed for no other reason than the absence of intelligence. With a public works project[26] that the Nazi party started, to put millions of Germans back to work

---

[25] Something complex is at risk of being a form of chaos. Simply because a thing is complex does not necessarily mean it has to be ordered, it can just have a lot of chaotic things occurring and the absence of order becomes apparent when examined closely, yet this chaos is complex all the same.

[26] Coincidentally, in 1933 President Franklin Roosevelt would implement as part of his New Deal, a similar public works project called the Public Works Administration to bring the United States out of its own Great Depression, unfortunately the systematic hate of a particular race accompanied his projects as well.

and help restore their economy, there then was no need to begin the systematic destruction of a single people. This idea of genocide was chaotic, and either chaos casts out order or order will cast out chaos. In Nazi Germany, chaos casted out order, mimicking its ousted foe with terrifying accuracy, so much so that in1936 the eleventh Olympiads were held there during this time. It is of no surprise that less than a century after emancipating slaves and four hundred years after their own attempted genocide on the natives of America, the United States government remained out of WWII until the war came to its naval base.

One would think that a nation built on the idea that all men are created equal would be the first to rescue the Jewish people if not for anything else other than the moral obligation to its own founding ideology. This would not be so. Just as Strom Thurmond would later put states' rights over human rights in his 1948 campaign speech, the U.S. government from 1933 until December 7, 1941, held the rights of a diabolical government in higher esteem than human rights. Remember the "Corporate Race"[27], a parent will protect its child, the king protects the prince, and corporations will protect corporations

---

[27] Refer to section II

the same way governments will protect governments to the detriment of the human race. We will again note at this particular junction that government is the parent of all corporations, so their blind eye behavior toward corporations and themselves should be of little to no surprise.

Let us briefly compare Nazi Germany's genocide and racism, in other words the product of hate, with the United States' genocide and racism up until the Civil Rights Act. The genocide of the natives to America along with the racism directed toward African slaves, their children African-American slaves, and their descendants black people can arguably be attributed to ancestral whites[28] hating each respective people for helping them survive and then helping them to

---

[28] There is no real terminology for this and it is with great difficulty to label this, but a necessity for this essay. To put it simply, all white people are not and were never all racist. However, some white people who are racist hide amongst their fellow white people masquerading as something they are not simply because they have the same skin as their contemporaries. The rest of white people are then misjudged simply because they are used as camouflage by these types of people amongst them just so racism can be perpetuated. Eventually this racist ideology pervades all people no matter what skin color because a game of "you act on your hate toward me so now I hate you and will soon act on that hate you have instilled in me against you as well" ensues. This leads to victory for all racist people and the defeat of the human race unless intelligence again is held with greater value than socialization. (The origins of racism no people will claim, so this idea is very controversial and complex, but for the purposes of this essay the preceding paragraph will suffice. However the author of this essay will revisit this topic of race in an entirely different works when the author can better articulate with better insight and understanding the full scope of this human dilemma.)

build a nation. Whether this help was forced or not is of no concern here and is a topic for an entirely different discussion. In contrast, the racism toward and genocide of the Jewish people in Nazi Germany can arguably be attributed to German Nazis hating them for what they saw as helping destroy their Fatherland. One can then argue that the U.S.'s hate toward the Natives, black people, and the ancestors of black people was attributed to creation while Nazi Germany's hate toward the Jewish people was attributed to destruction. Either way, not just this type of hate, but all hate is a form of chaos because it is destructive and a once a thing is destroyed it naturally enters a state of chaos until order is created, restoring it to its rightful state by ousting chaos.

If we were to look at the justice system and how they socialize the person they convict, we would see that they isolated the convicted person from society, confining them to a group of convicted persons the same as them, expecting some form of rehabilitation. This is no new discovery that by keeping people with the same type of people who exhibit same or similar behavior shared by both parties, that the same shared behavior will increase in skill, frequency, and severity. One of the claims that Albert Bandura's

Social Learning Theory makes is if you change a person's environment you can change their behavior and this is supposed to happen when a convicted person is giving time in the form of incarceration.

Before we go any further let us state that the justice system takes time from the convicted person under the false pretense that it is giving time when it sentences the convicted person. So before the convicted person even begins their sentence they must understand that their time of freedom is taking from them and a predetermined time of imprisonment is giving to them at an egregious exchange rate. Not only is time being taking, but also the opportunity for true rehabilitation. In its place is isolation from solutions and included in this place is the necessary tools for the perpetuation of what is deemed their deviant behavior. Now the place, this environment of the convicted person is definitely changed, but it is done so for the worse. By definition rehabilitation means, "the process of restoring an individual to a useful and constructive place in society especially through some form of vocational correctional or therapeutic retraining". Upon release, the ex-convict becomes more useful to the society he/she was taking from. The society being the deemed underworld of crime or the "illegal society" they lived in has now received its equivalency of a college graduate to better further this illegal society that the justice system has sworn to rid the law-abiding "legal society" of. With these two inextricably connected societies existing under one government the fallacies of law is once again on full display via the complex workings no one ever calls chaos. We will examine the reason for the rift and causation of this "illegal society" later in this section.

It is known that businessmen want cash and criminals want checks. For businessmen, the cash from the illegal society makes it easier for them to spend their money with no paper trail while for the criminal, checks from the legal society makes it easier for them to seem legitimized and spend their money without scrutiny from the law. Both societies share parallels, but government views them differently. Sociologist Jon Witt claims, "we do not regard killing in self-defense or in combat in the same way we view killing in cold blood…that is the case until we change our minds about how we view wartime killing." In this instance, murder is acceptable when justifiable by the law that governs the whole of legal society while it is distained by the legal society when considered done in "cold blood", and made punishable when it is done under the laws that govern the illegal society as a punishment for an offence in the illegal society. The constant in both cases is the act of killing. But the justification under the laws of the legal society is in conflict with the laws of nature and also those rules that govern the illegal society. "By the fundamental law of nature" John Locke wrote, "one may destroy a Man who makes War upon him." He went on to explain that, "using force, where he has no Right, to get me into his Power, let his pretence be what it will, I have no reason to suppose, that he, who would *take away my* liberty, would not when he had me in his Power, take away every thing else."

This brings us to the idea of the social contract and the supreme error in Rousseau's work in respect to the *Lawgiver*. He claims, "…each man must be stripped of his own powers, and given powers which are external to him, and which he cannot use without the help of others." In all cases the power he is stripped of is greater than external power which he receives in return from the lawgiver through the social contract for no other reason than this natural power is his birthright granted to him by nature. In Locke's view, the man who strips away another man/woman's power, their birthright "pretence be what it will", inevitably will destroy that person or the whole of a society who adheres to such demands by taking away everything from them, in effect permanently making them wards of the government. Rousseau continues by further arguing, "The nearer men's natural powers are to extinction or annihilation, and the stronger and more lasting their acquired powers, the stronger and more perfect is the social institution." In concluding this matter he states, "that if each citizen can do nothing whatever except through cooperation with others, and if the acquired power of the whole is equal to, or greater than, the sum of the natural power of each of the individuals, then we can say that law-making has reached the highest point of perfection."

The supreme error is the belief that if those hyper-intellectuals naturally born with charisma, high level intelligence, original thought and ideas, know-how to get people to follow them, all give up these facets of natural powers that most human beings are not capable of bringing out of themselves, then they, just as the rest, would be equally dependent on the next person and no one person will have any natural power over the next. Rousseau agrees or fails to realize that we are all human beings and by voluntarily giving up what is, through sheer existence, birthright, naturally yours, you are willingly entering a pact of servitude i.e. a social contract, subjecting ones-self to who or that which is perceived to be of "supreme intelligence". Rousseau sees that, "Gods would be needed to give men laws", yet it is man who gives man law through governments which men establish, ultimately leaving the men/women who do not relinquish their natural powers as the *Lawgivers,* who then view themselves as that "supreme intelligence", to those who either, one, foolishly relinquished their natural powers for the perfection of law-making or two, never had it to begin with. There is a third, those who have natural powers and refused to give them up for the perfection of law-making and it is those who refused, who became the outlaws of legal society and the builders of the illegal society that coexists by necessity for the legal society to waywardly function as it does. For without illegality how can there be legality and without legality, why would the system exist?

These people are those who knew, as Locke further suggested, that those who would take away your liberty would just as soon take everything else including life from you. It is then the flaw of the social contract that human beings willfully condemn themselves under the pretense they are gaining more power than they are giving up. But by giving up one of those unalienable rights, this time *liberty*, they are also admitting they no longer are capable of governing themselves even in the most miniscule of matters and this is the actual reason for the rift mentioned earlier in this section separating the legal society from the deemed illegal society. Those in the illegal society feel they can govern themselves while those in the legal society feel that their law is the needed and only governance.

Through this admittance, the government, who ultimately turns out to be the lawgiver, does everything that Locke supposes. The title of illegal is then giving so as to demonize those who walk in this way in the eyes of those who so hastily Esau'd[29] themselves' with no serious contemplation, to reassure the Esau'd that by partaking in the social contract that they made the right decision. The right decision, in the eyes of the now exposed lawgiver, being the forfeiture of the people's natural power, their birthright, now allowing them participation with others like them in the socialization of humanity, is made.

---

[29] Genesis 25: versus 29-34

The parallels of both societies are never more apparent than through their tax systems. Legal society pays income tax and it is the legal society who calls the illegal society's tax, extortion. If we were to define the two we would see virtually no difference in their meanings. A tax is the lawful appropriation of moneys from the people by government used for the needs of the people along with the maintenance and functioning of said government. Extortion is the unlawful or forced appropriation of funds from the people for the maintenance and functioning of an organization that may or may not use these funds on the people they were appropriated from. Lawful and unlawful are the differences in these definitions.

When government officials use tax dollars for their own personal gain this is referred to as a misappropriation of funds and corruption is to be blamed on this "isolated incident". When a deemed illegal organization uses its appropriated funds to better a community it is seen as an "isolated incident" used to launder money and not the norm. The point is that both societies are guilty of the same thing and the idea that an illegal organization is just that, illegal, brings us back to the false statement mentioned earlier that these outlaws in the illegal society are not capable of governing themselves even in the most miniscule of matters. However, this idea is perpetuated[30] by laws that either force the savage behavior, or force the outlaw into conforming by stripping away his/hers' own power and accepting that lessened power which is granted through the process of socialization, by the lawgivers who never relinquished their power to begin with and convinced a greater portion of the whole of humanity that servitude is better than true independence so long ago.

With two opposing forces existing under one government, chaos is now the norm while order has not only become unrecognizable, but when identified, is immediately scorned and discredited. If intelligence had held its place over socialization, this devolving into chaos which has been misconstrued as something other than what it is, as was the case with 1936 Germany, would actually be evolving into a higher form of order. The rise of chaos

---

[30] To illustrate this point, one has only to study the Mexican Drug War fought by the US government in conjunction with the Mexican government and one will see the increase of violence between cartels and against both governments has a direct correlation with the passage of more stringent drug laws, the increase in seizures, the questionable tactics used to infiltrate these organizations, and widespread corruption. Corruption in the cartels in the form of informants, and corruption in the governments in the form of bribery, as well as informants who keep the cartels abreast as to what each government is doing, and the questionable tactics used in defeating these businessmen on the other side of the law.

through the misplacement of socialization is achieved due to the innate need of connection to insure ones' survival that comes from the designated duality that makes up the singularity, which is the individual human being. In other words, one plus one equals one, meaning it takes one man and one woman to create at least one child. Each human is therefore equal parts man, and equal parts woman.

This idea, which will no doubt prove controversial in the near, but correct in the distant future, furthers the idea of homosexuality being completely normal. If a person is comprised of both male and female then it is completely feasible and acceptable that they may be attracted to either the same, opposite, or both sexes depending on which equal part refused to relinquish its power. *The victor of this confrontation then becomes the "sexual orientation lawgiver" writing its' own "genetic social contract" for the human body.* Under the aforementioned standards human beings are wired to need connection, no matter the reason, either to procreate, for physical/emotional companionship, for a sense of community, or for protection, this need is apparent. Even in religions that seem at odds in their belief we see the need as well. In Al-'Ankabut it reads, "We believe what has been sent down to us, and we believe what has been sent down to you. Our God and your God is one.[31]"

If we were to examine Locke's treatment of Adam in his first treatise we are to find that he, "cannot see, nor consequently understand, how a Supposition of Natural Freedom is a denial Adam's Creation." It is here were will attempt to clarify and give some understanding on how Adam's creation denies all suppositions of natural freedom, why natural freedom can only exist by the denial of his creation, and why socialization becomes necessity through Adam's creation.

To understand why natural freedom cannot exist because of the creation of Adam, we must first understand to what purpose was Adam's creation for and to do so we must start at the very beginning of the bible and see how God created all things therein. God created the world using the spoken word, "And God said, let there be light: and there was light."[32] It never specifies any other method used, only that, "God said." Later, in the book of John, the writer tells us that, "In the beginning was the Word and the Word was with God, and the

<hr>

[31] The Koran 29:46
[32] Genesis 1:3

Word was God". This portion tells us where the Word had been, who the Word was with at the time, and who the Word was. It also says that in God was life and that this life was the light of men, however when this light was shown to darkness, the darkness did not comprehend it.

Further, it says two important things to the creation of Adam which will be stated now and explained in greater detail shortly after, for the connections are not so clearly apparent. In the book of John it explains that John was not the light, but came to bear witness to the light and the first important thing reads "That was the true Light, which lighteth every man that cometh into the world." The second important thing reads, "And the Word was made flesh, and dwelt among us, (and we beheld his glory as of the only begotten of the Father,), full of grace and truth."[33] Illustrated in these few biblical verses is the oft overlooked portion of the story of Jesus. From these verses it is understood that Jesus was the Word in flesh. Yet if Jesus was the Word, which is what proceeds out of one's mouth, in this case, the mouth belonging to God, then he is indeed the Word of God. If we look deeper, it can be further understood that if the Word

---

[33] The Book of John Ch. 1

was used to create all things, then Jesus, though not in fleshly form, was at the beginning and the Word of God, can be found in all things created.

Even looking deeper in the text, we can deduce that the Word, when spoken by God not only created, but also put light into all humans. However, the true Light was Jesus, the Word in flesh, who dwelt amongst humans who all had the light in them hence the reason all humans are called the children of God. They are called so because there is a piece of that light in every human. A piece of God being in each one, clarifies why all humans can be saved and we need look no further than Thomas Hobbes words on the laws of nature mentioned earlier in section II to understand why, "man is forbidden to do that, which is destructive of his life." Since God said, "Let us make man in our image, after our likeness: and let them have dominion"[34] it can be further deduced that if man is created in God's likeness and image, then it is a law of God that God not to do that which would prove destructive to God, so if a piece of God is in each human, then God has to allow them to be saved in order to prevent being destructive to God's self. This process is called the

---

[34] Genesis 1:26

"Redemption Plan" by believers of God, because it is meant to redeem the pieces of God, the light placed in human beings, which have become as rotten fruit in God's garden, the Earth, from rotten the rest of the fruit, ultimately leading God to destroy the whole of the garden, to the temporary detriment, not the death of God's self as Nietzsche would have.

So the Word was sent as flesh in the form of Jesus to show all humans what adhering to God's Word will allow one to do, only if one submits and obeys with the rest of God's children to the *heavenly social contract* inherently understood through God's creation of the world and as the apostle Paul wrote on the gentiles who knew not God or of his law but were doers of the same, "these, having not the law, are a law unto themselves: Which shew the work of the law written in their hearts."[35] Before we get to Adam and the garden we will conclude this matter on the lesser told story of Jesus by using his words to describe him-self and show how they are applicable to the preceding paragraph. We turn again our gaze to the book of John where Jesus spoke saying, "I am the way, the truth, and the life: no man cometh unto the father, but by me."[36] He is the way,

---

[35] Romans 2:14-15

for by the Word is the way the world and everything therein was created, he is the truth because it is truth which with he is filled, and he is the life because life is the light that is in all humans and it is through this connection, light, that all humans liveth, through Jesus, who is the Word in flesh, which traced back, is the Word that proceeded out of the mouth of God, which ultimately is the source from which all things spring forth.

Pertaining to Adam, the first man to become a living soul, who from which all souls in human beings bare likeness, was given a charge for these reasons. As the soul was neither living nor dead prior to Adam's being, subsequently he and his descendant's would not be the same as those things created which were not imparted with a living soul and this distinguished Adam from man and beast in likeness and in law. To demonstrate why this is possible we will dissect both processes of man's creation within the bible.

The first process occurs when God says to the unknown others, "Let us make man in our image". This first creation of man is done in the open with the unknown others[37] aware of man's creation.

---

[36] The Book of John 14:6

[37] We will refer to the "us" as the unknown others simply because the "us" either means God was schizophrenic during creation or some other being(s) was

After this petition for the creation of man is giving to the unknown others it reads, "So God created man in his own image, in the image of God created he him; male and female created he them." In this first account of man's creation the unknown others were aware and by their silence consented to the creation of man i.e. humans male and female.

Now the second time God does not create a man, he forms a man and it is done without the consent or petition to no unknown others, it is just done by God's own council. It reads, "...and there was not a man to till the ground...And the Lord God formed man of the dust of the ground, and breathed into his nostrils the breathe of life; and man became a living soul. And the Lord God planted a garden eastward in E'den; and there he put the man whom he had formed...God took the man, and put him into the garden of E'den to dress it and to keep it."[38] The charge this man, who was not named by God as such, but we are told whose name was Adam was to tend

---

present at the time.

[38] Genesis Ch. 1- 2: This entails great intricacy, so as not to overburden the reader, the significance of the mist going up and watering the earth before Adam's creation and no watering of the Earth before man's creation will be left out as it will take up a book in itself and that topic is not the purpose of nor does it help or take away from this essay.

to a garden. The humans' male and female created earlier, who God did not breathe the breath of life into, were given dominion over everything in the Earth, and was also told to, "Be fruitful, and multiply and replenish the Earth and subdue it." We will return to this idea of being fruitful and multiplying shortly as well as to Adam, but for now we will look at what we will refer to as, "God's Dilemma" as this, although it may cause certain readers to become apoplectic, is within reason to take a serious consideration to its contents.

This dilemma that God presents himself with begins with the moment God decides to form a man and make him a living soul without consulting the unknown others that God petitioned when the first humans, male and female were created by he. Not only did God form a man without petitioning the unknown others, God breathed into him the "breathe of life" making him a "living soul", something that the earlier humans male and female were not, in effect creating a monarch in Adam, who, by his existence had divinity in a human body and by which divine right was granted through that piece of God that the earlier humans did not receive. It was the time between the creation of the humans male and female and before the formation of Adam that God makes a choice. To form a man in secret without consulting these unknown others or to let the male and female already created have the unchallenged dominion over the Earth that was their right at the time was God's options.

Prior to the formation of Adam, there was no choice, only what was said and what was done through the said word, order, to be specific. God spoke what was to be done and it was done. After the formation of Adam, we find that God begins to give reasons for his orders, along with the first don't, a break in a succession of many do's, "God commanded the man saying, Of every tree of the garden thou mayest freely eat: But of the tree of the knowledge of good and evil thou shalt not eat of it: for in the day that thou eatest thereof thou shalt surely die."

Instead of giving Adam true dominion over everything as was giving to the humans male and female who were created, Adam is allowed everything "but". It is this "but" that constitutes the freewill giving to Adam as God demonstrated his own freewill, the means by which God's dilemma occurred, by the creation of Adam without petitioning the unknown others. This is so, because the breath of life that was breathed into Adam contained that thing, freewill, that made God choose to form him without the unknown others being petitioned and that same thing, freewill, is what was giving to Adam which in turn was then giving to Eve, becoming the causation behind her accepting the serpent's words as truth.

In all things created outside of humans i.e. male and female, God just "said" and it was done, no choice, no freewill. The petition alone to the unknown others then puts humans in higher regards than all prior creations and this sets up the hierarchical structure we see. Having Adam, the first man to become a living soul as the divine monarch under God, humans male and female being granted dominion over everything created under this divine monarch, and all things created before both the divine monarch and humans' male and female subjected to the will of all the aforementioned beings. So God created from the bottom up and from the top, reigns the monarch Adam, as everything was created for him, as his natural realm.

As to Eve's encounter with the serpent, we have to ask to what purpose did the serpent presented his proposal to her? It would seem that God's dilemma became known to the unknown others and it was they who sent the serpent to Eve, who, by being the first to be imparted with a piece of Adam's living soul, did not show the same resilience as Adam would have if he'd been presented the same proposal. This is only so because God spoke the order directly to Adam and not Eve, who received not only the order, but her portion of Adam's living soul, who was but only separated from humans male and female through a breath, second-hand. So her need to follow the order giving was lesser than Adam's from the way which she received the order, in essence leaving her blameless.

Eve's encounter with the serpent reads as follows, "And the serpent said unto the woman, Ye shall not surely: For God doth know that in the day ye eat thereof, then your eyes shall be opened and ye shall be as gods knowing good and evil. And when the woman saw that the tree was good for food, and pleasant to the eyes and a tree to be desired to make one wise, she took of the fruit thereof, and did eat and gave also to her husband with her, and he did eat."[39] It is after they eat the fruit of the tree that they gain self-awareness and become naked and ashamed, a stark contrast to their prior being just naked and not ashamed. From here we can attribute

---

[39] It is an interesting observation that the serpent is the first to speak to Eve while it is God who is the first to speak to Adam.

the saying, "Ignorance is bliss", as both were in bliss before Eve's encounter with the serpent and it would seem that ignorance is simply the lack of knowledge of good and evil.

Now God's dilemma becomes Adam and Eve's dilemma because the external choice, singular, that was giving to them by God has now become internalized choices, plural, within both of their respective living souls due to the ingestion of the fruit from the tree of knowledge of good and evil. The first choice, to eat of the tree of knowledge of good and evil or not, being external to Adam because it was spoke to him by God while Eve's choice was already internalized by the way she was made. This was one of the reasons why the serpent chose her over Adam. The second choice, to either clothe ones' self or not was internalized because God did not speak directly to either Eve or Adam in regards to clothing themselves or not, hence the first internalized decision was simultaneously made by Adam and Eve, a decision which has been continually practiced throughout human history. Their decision was to cover themselves, in other words provide protection for themselves from one another. The first form of protection is protection of ones' body from another and the first awareness of another's body is through sight, so the first thing they both did to protect their privacy one from the other was sew fig leaves together and made themselves aprons to cover their bodies. This act not only was an act of protecting their privacy, one from the other, but it also signified the act of ownership over one's body, in turn creating yet another choice as to whether or not to share ones' body with another or not.

To the issue of whether or not the serpent deceived Eve by lying to her, it is not an issue at all. The serpent did not lie or beguile her. It is therefore not an issue of lying or beguilement, for the serpent did neither. The issue lies in the understanding of the living soul. The soul, as mentioned earlier in this section was neither living nor dead prior to Adam. It simply was within God, who exists, being Alpha and Omega, the one, without being subjected to life or death unless so chosen. Therefore, the soul, when put into existence outside the body of God into another body must become living in order for it to have the option of being destroyed, in other words for it to die. This is predicated on the time God had between the creation of humans male and female and the formation of Adam, the first man to be imparted with a living soul. The serpent, being sent by the unknown others, would then be dealing with the knowledge of this information and in knowing as much, spoke to Eve from this level of understanding of the soul, which she held a piece of within her, a fact she was ignorant to, but the serpent was well aware of and this negates any interpretation of the serpent's words as lies.

We find that God, upon discovery of Adam's disobedience, put Adam and Eve out of the garden and forced them to till the ground outside the garden from whence he was formed as Adam was not formed in the garden, but placed in after his formation. It is here, before this banishment that we find God speaking to the unknown others again and the true reason Adam and Eve were put out of the garden of E'den is brought to light, "Behold, the man is become as one of us, to know good and evil: and now, lest he put forth his hand, and take also of the tree of life, and eat, and live for ever."[40] It is only after Adam has become a step closer to God and the unknown others through the eating of the fruit from the tree of the knowledge of good and evil that God petitions them again. In their silence, again they consent to God's decision.

So "God's dilemma" was the fact that Adam had gained the knowledge that God and the unknown others already possessed and

---

[40] Genesis 3:22-23

it was because God had chosen to form a man with a living soul without petitioning the unknown others that this happened in the first place. God's solution to this dilemma would ultimately be his "Redemption Plan", which was in place well before God chose to form Adam and breathe the breath of life into him simply because he used his Word to create all things save for Adam, who he formed using dust, hence Adam being the anomaly. It is then for this reason that Adam's creation denies natural freedom. Adam was Gods' flaw and in being as such God had to correct this mistake. Further, natural freedom did exist, but only for those humans' male and female who were granted dominion over the earth prior to the formation of Adam. This is because having dominion gave them the freedom to do what they liked in and to the environment which they existed, nature, and this in itself is natural freedom for they knew of no other form of nature, being denied nothing, as Adam was because he was imparted with a living soul and charged to tend the garden of E'den. A charge the humans male and female were not giving because they were not imparted with a living soul. They were not giving any "don'ts" as Adam was either, in fact they were encouraged to procreate and to procreate in abundance, a punishment however for

Eve, "I will greatly multiply thy sorrow and thy conception; in sorrow thy shalt bring forth children."[41] Once Adam and Eve were put out the garden and began the process of socialization with these humans male and female and began to procreate with them, they as well lost their natural freedom. Socialization then becomes a necessity, for all who now are imparted with pieces of the living soul originally imparted in Adam when God breathed the breath of life into him without petitioning the unknown others, in order for God's "Redemption Plan" to work. Thus the divinity of Adam and the living soul he was imparted with now is dispersed throughout all of humanity and every human then believes they have the same divine right as he. So Nietzsche was off, God is not dead, God is simply flawed. If we are to deny the existence of God and by doing so deny the creation of Adam then we can presuppose that the only true thing is natural freedom, void of any obligation to any sovereign either divine or human. The only laws then that govern will be by those who impose their will on their fellow humans all in the name of protecting and preserving ones' self which is what the animals do.

---

[41] Genesis 3:15-16

It has been misunderstood that the laws of nature govern both man and animal alike, but this is not so. Great distress has been giving to the human race because of this misunderstanding. What humans have considered the laws of nature; those laws which the basis of so much of our civility lies, are actually laws of animals and being as such should only be adhered to by animals. Through the adherence to these archaic laws such as self-preservation and survival of the fittest we are no more-better than the savage beasts, the lion and the wolf. We greet violence with violence albeit delayed in reaction, via war or through the act of death in the form of a penalty. We are territorial, sectioning off what has been already sectioned by nature. For those who offend the law we isolate them from the rest of civilized society in hopes they will returned civil or return not at all. To ensure our continued evolution we must distance ourselves from these beastly laws which animals live by and cease calling them the laws of nature, for they are as much laws of nature as driving a car is to a dead snail.

If intelligence were to take its rightful place above socialization this would be a well-deserved and much needed restart or at least as Hayek wrote a *"reculer pour mieux sauter."*[42]

Destruction is the path which chaos travels and history has proven time and again what results socialization has garnered humanity. For every ingenious advancement humanity has made throughout history, it has been preceded by an equal, if not greater, trail of blood or some foolish act(s) of which the perpetrator denies or narrowly apologizes for, usually with no reciprocity involved unless it benefits those in power, who maintain society to their sole benefit. Through socialization, society is in effect a contradiction because it is comprised of a collective of tax paying people who have ownership over their own personal dominion, family, house, car, business or whatever they have gained through socialization, yet these very same people are supposed to learn from those around them while at the same time learning how to live with those around them. How then can this be accomplished when you and the people you are learning from and learning to live with, are vying for the same thing to allow each other to acquire what is needed to gain ownership of the aforementioned possessions from a limited supply of said possessions and that of the currency needed to pay taxes and

---

[42] Latin roughly translated meaning to take a step back in order to increase the distance of one's jump

purchase said possessions, without eventually having the opposing imposing wills' of one another infringe on those inalienable rights bestowed upon each and everyone one of us by our creator? The answer for those who agree with socialization would be socialization, and through the process of socialization we are to learn these answers. The problem then becomes socialization itself. For through this process of learning from and learning how to live with each other we are perpetuating the problems we are trying to solve due to socialization and this in itself presents the contradiction that is socialization.

It can then be surmised that Rousseau was right in his suggestion that the natural state for humans is solitude[43]. But how then would humanity advance beyond the level of beast if woman and man met only to procreate? This would imply that we are nothing more than mere savage beasts concerned only with our survival, negating our advancement, consequentially leaving succeeding generations in the same state as every generation preceding them, simply surviving by being the fittest. We are not as such. We are as Ayn Rand wrote, "those who give material form to

---

[43] A reference to Rousseau's work, "Discourse on Inequality"

thoughts, and reality to value", and being as such we shall succeed immeasurably in doing. In order to do so, we must first replace socialization with the communicable intelligence and solely communicable intelligence which will bring forth a higher form of order. By communicating only that which is intelligent and abhorring the communication of mass ignorance can this be achieved. Sadly we exist in the technological age where the internet allows for the communication of mass ignorance at a higher rate than that which is intelligent is communicated.

V

It would seem from the prior sections that this essay is against any form of collectivism. However, this is contraire to the point. The idea that production is for use and not for profit is indeed correct in thought and in practice, but has proven to be greatly flawed in its implementation. This is in part due to those who claimed divine right as well as those who claim the right to be lawgivers who are in positions to implement the proper practice of collectivism. Who instead, then implement, to their advantage, a form of collectivism that reroutes the profits from production, in use and monetary gain, back to themselves neglecting the whole of the people the production is meant for simply because the "I" is the architect of such production while the "We" is the means by which the production is done. This can be interpreted as individualism by way of the "I" without "We", not before "We", no, just "I" without any "We", eliminating the collective for what the "I" see as their just and deserved gain becoming rightfully theirs' by way of conquest or in rare cases, the actual inception of an idea.

It is individualism, being what humanity cannot afford to practice, as the "I" becomes the metaphorical soul that inhabits the body of the artificial man and all those who claim divinity or the like, in the form of lawgiver i.e. government, or architect of production i.e. the corporation or oppressor to those who care not for such titles or way of living. Those who care not's lack of concern for such matters only indicates that they view not themselves as lesser, equal, or greater than their fellow humans, but as one with the whole of humanity, a trait that consistently proves detrimental to them. For it is too many "I" that fail to understand that they are in a symbiotic relationship with the "We". Yet it is far too many "We", much more than the "I" who fail to understand, that do not know the meaning of a symbiotic relationship.

Therefore neither reaps the true benefits of such a relationship. In fact they suffer in the areas where they should gain the most in this symbiotic relationship. The reason for such relationships in humanity as Hobbes wrote is that, "men, for the atteyning of peace, and conservation of themselves thereby, have made an Artificiall Man, which we call a Common-wealth; so also have they made Artificiall Chains, called Civll Lawes, which they themselves, by mutuall covenants, have fastned at one end, to the lips of that Man, or Assembly, to whom they have given the Soveraigne Power; and at the other end to their own ears." It is this artificial man in all of his forms albeit, government, corporation, or nation etc., who by way of his existence has no other choice but to immediately begin subjugating humanity at the behest of the "I" who are themselves very much a part of humanity. The question then becomes are the "I" aware that their doing is not only their undoing, but the undoing of the whole of humanity?

In all things mentioned as of yet in this essay, from government, to corporations, even the idea of socialization, they all have the same common denominator, human beings. So when it is said of corporations that they are evil or that government is bad what is really being said is being said about human beings. For these artificial men are only what we make them, which is nothing more than a reflection of their creators. What part then do human beings play in their own oppression if not the role of oppressor? There, as of yet have been no otherworldly enemy oppressing the whole of humanity, only humanity divided against itself that proves its worst enemy. And only in the wake of an attack from the great enemy terrorism, is the whole of a society united on one accord, which is no more than a small portion of the whole of humanity. We find that unity amongst humans is only achieved in the shadows cast by the great enemy. This is likely due to the fact that in shadows it is harder to see one another because all are fighting, in darkness, this common great enemy to find light as to rid themselves of this shadow. When the great enemy is temporarily defeated and light is once again found, the faces of those fighting beside one another are exposed and the realization of whom your allies were and that the great enemy is temporarily vanquished settles in. With no great enemy to keep the whole united, lesser enemies are than fabricated from the now exposed allies and the whole that once was becomes temporarily vanquished along with the great enemy. It is the view of the "We" and that of the "I" needing to be changed if collectivism and individualism is to benefit the whole humanity instead of being a gain for one at the expense of another.

What may seem as counterintuitive is the only way to correct the conflict of the "I" versus the "We" and to unite the collectivist and the individualist once and for all. This thing that is on the surface counterintuitive is the death of the "We". At this, the "I" shall rejoice, but they too must suffer not only the same fate as the "We", but at the same exact time as well. So how is the death of the "I" and "We" achieved? It is one thing to say what must be done, yet it is another to explain how it is done. The "We" is the product of socialization and since socialization is a contradiction, the "We" is at constant war with itself over the great enemy terrorism. The pretense by which the "We" came to be was false to begin with so in truth the "We" is as real as the artificial man, whose existence depends on both the "We" and the "I" belief in it.

If there is no belief in the artificial man then the artificial man along with his artificial chains ceases to exist and the option of creating another means of self-subjugation or the creation of a higher form of order can be discussed. So the "We" exist because of the belief that each individual human being has in it. Inspired by the great enemy terrorism, which is not a person but an idea turned to action, an action being in the physical or psychological form, the "We" finds itself in a cyclical war with itself without end. To the "I" this is nothing more than an endless means of production because the war is against ideas which are intangible unless turned to action and therefore can be perpetuated with minimal questioning as long as these ideas are only turned to action periodically. Once an idea has been created it cannot be destroyed. An idea can become many things, but it cannot be destroyed and this is what connects it to energy and why ideas are so dangerous, specifically the idea of terrorism. It inspires fear which is nothing more than a reaction to a perceived threat or danger, the threat and danger not necessarily having to actually exist.

Now to the death of the "We", it occurs in that short window where the great enemy is defeated and the united "We" come from under the temporarily defeated great enemy's shadow into the light and see their exposed allies. Then in this moment the "We" dies. From individual human beings is the "We" formed and to individual human beings the "We" returns. The "We" dies simply because that which united it temporarily ceases to exist and the fear inspired by terrorism, a thing that cannot be destroyed, is now displayed on the individual faces of each human being that make up the "We". Fearing it-self, the "We" splinters and becomes the very same thing that created its constant warring, the "I". It becomes the "I" because it is the "I" who are the architects of production, those who give material form to thoughts, separating themselves from the "We" through such actions. Protecting themselves from themselves as Eve and Adam protected themselves one from the other. Hence the "We" protects it-self by separating from it-self, creating the "I". It is then in this same moment that the "We" dies, that the "I" dies as well. It dies simply because it has become the "We" by way of the aforementioned splintering of the "We". From the "We" the "I" is formed and to the "We" the "I" returns.

A moment of clarity occurs when both the "I" and "We" are dead. They are one in the same, they are all human beings comprising but only one race, the human race and it is the human race that must be seen as one individual, a leviathan among the stars. Unlike the romanticized capitalist credo "I will stop the motor of the world", spoken by John Galt in Ayn Rand's Atlas Shrugged, the motor will indeed continue to run. If it is not the "I" versus the "We" it will be the proletariat versus the bourgeoisie or the democrats versus republicans etc. It is these outward struggles between ideologies[44] played out among the human race that are nothing more

---

[44] With the exception of racism which is hate in its unadulterated form. It is likened to the bull that goes mad over the color red, which is acceptable, for the bull is but an animal. So what is a human who goes mad over the color of another human if not anything more than an animal who is exhibiting animal behavior?

than the manifestations of the inner struggles within the individual human being. From the consummation of two comes one. One man plus one woman equals one child[45]. The child, being comprised of two separate wholes is therefore in itself a conflict unto itself upon creation. In laymen's terms meaning, either being human is being the problem, or being human is being the solution.

---

[45] Reference section IV

"I sacrifice myself to my love, *and my neighbor as myself*"— so goes the language of all creators. But all creators are hard. Thus spoke Zarathustra.

VI

What is it that keeps society tied together on a global scale if not capital? Socialization stands on its own merit for better or worse, yet it is capitalism, the perpetually unsatisfied thirst and hunger for currency and capital gains by humans and corporations alike, that has always been the undercurrent in the ocean of socialization. Both the "I" and the "We" desire currency, if not for want, then by necessity alone to exist in this ever expanding society. Yet it is the corporation that needs capital to survive and it is for this reason it so fiendishly acquires capital with no regard for human life.

A human society that has permeated nearly every part of the Earth with no remorse and forces every indigenous people it comes in contact with to enter into its enterprise of socialization or die, has been fooled by its own invention capital which, as it turns out, has no practical function for the individual human, but is the nourishment that allows for the growth of the government king and the corporation prince. In fact, Jean Baudrillard suggested that "capital…is a challenge to society." As mentioned at the beginning of this essay, capitalism in its Darwinian form is what we now see on a global scale. If the laws of nature state that it is the survival of the fittest, then by all accounts the laws of capitalism must state that it is the survival of the richest. And who is richer than the corporation or better worded the corporate race? The latter law is as illogical as the law of nature because currency is not the equivalent of labor it has no practical use save for the exchange for labor. It is currency that negates the actualization of labor for labor's sake and hinders true human progress by rewarding those who give more value to currency than to the actual labor or laborer. In essence it is an extra step in a simple process. The price the consumer pays must reflect the true cost of production. However, the true cost of production is not reflected in the consumer's price so the true cost is a false equivalency while the actual cost reflects greed, the corporation's need to be fed profit. Basically currency's only equivalence is socialization, for both are continually giving value by that which has no value itself, yet devalues everything which it interacts with, the corporation.

There isn't anything that generates greater capital than a corporation. It is the corporation that produces the currency which helps fuel its own capital, that individual humans work and strive for, and in turn insures the corporate race's existence and survival. In the end this currency departs from the individual human who possesses it and returns to its place of origin, the corporation, and adds to the corporation's capital gains. Even when a corporation suffers a loss of capital the capital rarely trickles down in the form of currency to the individual human. Instead it goes to another member of the corporate race. So if Ford suffers a loss of profits it is only because Toyota has gained. If it is not because Toyota has gained then the individual human has spent their currency with some other non-motor corporation. Either way, even if Ford suffers losses due solely to its own mismanagement or failure on its own part, the currency returns back to some corporation, even when it is being

burned after it is taking out of circulation. So what we are beginning

to see again, as we have witnessed throughout history, is the

interactions between races. Only this time it is the human race

interacting with our creation the corporate race and the deciding

factor for the victor and apex participant in this

interaction/relationship has become technology, as it has been for

some time now.

Humans have ceased evolving if in fact we have ever evolved[46]

outside the evolution of human thought, which is proven by the

various advancements in the arts and sciences etc., all being results

of human thought. Since humans are not evolving outside of thought,

we have turned to evolving technology, a thing that we have

---

[46] We are supposedly to have evolved from bacteria yet it continually evolves whenever threatened. For example penicillin is already on at least its 4th generation in part due to the bacteria it was meant to destroy evolving and adapting to resist it. The same is seen in viruses such as influenza which grows resistant seasonally to its vaccinations. Not only do the aforementioned evolve, they do so at a faster rate compared to the millennia that humans allegedly take to evolve and adapt to their environment. This is puzzling due to the fact that the environment humans are adapting to is constantly changing. Raising the question "how could humans have evolved if what they were evolving for was constantly changing?" Evolution then becomes detrimental to humanity, acting almost as a saboteur because it is at least (purposely or not) one step behind the ever changing environment. Proof of this is evolution has never provided any species protection against humanity i.e. the dodo bird, but to the laymen this is negated by the idea of "survival of the fittest".

constantly evolved to the point where technology is almost autonomous and a few generations away of being able to evolve and reproduce itself. In other words, technology is a few generations from being human or at least human-esque.

The corporation, capitalism, and technology have become virtually inseparable in motive and in their being, three heads connected to a common body, humanity. As previously stated, humanity has ceased evolving and instead turned to evolving its technology, quite possible to its detriment, while the corporation continues to master the art of capitalism. The three now act as the heads of a cerebus, guarding humanity from what else if not humanity? If the common body shared is humanity and it is guarding against itself, then humanity has become as the mad dog chasing its own tail. This cerebus mistakes its own tail for that of another, consequentially running in a circle repeating its history in a cyclical pattern over and over from one generation to the next indefinitely.

This suggests some form of mental illness, a global version schizophrenia, a type of hebetude of sorts. A mental game is played allowing this mythological savage beast from the realm of the supernatural to enter into the natural realm where the individual human is reduced to nothing more than mere savage beasts, the lion and the wolf. With no natural enemy, this three headed hell hound ultimately ravages an unsuspecting ecosystem that it is not native to and proceeds to destroy its ill-prepared inhabitants. Similar in the way that the American crayfish did the river Thymes in England or the anaconda in the Florida everglades, this cerebus mirrors the same. We have seen this cerebus be the cause of oil spills (Exxon Valdez oil spill 1989 and BP oil spill in 2010), computer dump sites such as Guiyu, China, instigators of domestic war like DeBeers buying of conflict diamonds in Angola, and nuclear melt downs such as Three Mile Island in 1979 or the more devastating Chernobyl in 1986.

All the aforementioned were destructive to our ecosystem, some resulting in the senseless deaths of humans. So the effects of this theoretical cerebus on the natural realm are far removed from theory and indeed very much real. However, when this cerebus faces it-self in the mirror it does not see a three headed beast connected to humanity, it sees the reflection of a one headed leviathan[47], the

[47] Reference Section II

corporate race, standing on its own merit separate from the human race. Technology and capital are now imbued within the corporation whereas when technology and capital are in the possession of humanity it is simply used as a means. This is the advantage the corporate race has over the human race. Technology does not evolve faster than the corporation instead it evolves with it. Humans, if we do evolve, do so at a slower rate than the evolution of technology. So what use to be assets for humanity; corporations, capitalism, and technology have now become not only a liability, but a danger to humans, again[48] viz. the created is greater than the creator.

For all intended purposes the corporation is nothing more than a sociopath exhibiting criminal behavior. What then does this say about the corporation's creators? Further, what does this say that humans allow government, the parent of all corporations to rule over society? Humanity has in fact placed a sociopathic entity in a governing position of power over itself, hoping to one day have this sociopath rule over the whole of humanity, not just separate parts of humanity. In this way we can begin to discuss, as Baudrillard suggested, how capital is a challenge to society. Now since the

---

[48] Reference Section III

proposer of this challenge has been identified as the corporate race and the ecosystem they have been introduced to is not their own then maybe capital should be viewed as detrimental to the human race, but in truth, beneficial only to the corporate race. Let us reexamine the relationship between the "We" and the "I" before continuing. For it was the subjugation of the "We", in this instance those who first traversed that ocean from England due to religious persecution, by the monarchal "I" that sparked the idea of the American dream, life, liberty and the pursuit of happiness.

Before these pilgrims could even reach the shores of the land that would become America they signed what is known as the Mayflower Compact. This document announced the advancement of their Christian faith, the glory of their God, and honor of their country and king. The country, and king in title, they would soon disavow and dishonor in a little over a century. A document also stating that theirs' was a, "voyage to plant the first colony…and combine ourselves together into a civill body politick, for our better ordering and preservation." It was the drafting of this document aboard the Mayflower that took this "We" and transformed them into the "I" before they even encountered the natives of this foreign land.

By signing this document they became to the unsuspecting natives that which they themselves so desperately fled from. Maybe even worse than the monarchal "I" due to the fact theirs' was a roving entity that willingly went into this social contract, each being a witness to the other after seeing what a social contract had previously imposed upon them. It then becomes this social contract that allowed these pilgrims, by definition, those who journey far as an act of religious devotion, to unequivocally implement everything stated in their social contract called the Mayflower Compact on these natives, making them the "I"[49] to the natives who were now the "We".

Interestingly enough, as Hobbes stated about the conservation (another word for preservation) of one's self, and to achieve peace, the people will create an artificial man i.e. a government as the means to that peace and this is what those pilgrims did aboard the Mayflower. So the pilgrims who fled their land as the persecuted "We" entered a foreign land, social contract in tow, as the persecuting "I". A native people who knew not these

---

[49] It was the Uniformity Act of 1559 that led the puritans to separate from the Church of England, the We separating from the I.

pilgrims' God, ways, motives, or technology would succumb to the same for no other reason than believing that the "We" can convert the "I".

It was the grave mistake of the native "We" to show the foreign "I" how to survive on their land. A thing as simple as showing them how to properly grow and harvest crops still has its ramifications today. For the "I", are those who want smaller government, are in favor of big business i.e. corporations, privatization, little to no regulation, a free market in every sense of the term, in a nut shell, Darwinian capitalism. The "I" are the proverbial soul, even if it is not admitted, of the government king and the corporation prince. From the native "We" showing the pilgrims, the "I", how to grow corn, to a little over three hundred years later an American human cannot grow corn without purchasing seeds, which are only good for one season, from a corporation that has genetically modified the seeds to increase their profits.

An example of one such corporation is Monsanto[50]. Monsanto has a gene patent that the United States Supreme Court continues to uphold which allows the corporation to sue, and win,

[50] Supreme Court case Bowman v. Monsanto Co.

anyone who grows crops from their seeds, without purchase, either on purpose or inadvertently, even if the wind blows said seeds. The implications of this are terrifying. What these Supreme Court decisions mean is that Monsanto can, under law, possibly one day very soon own all the crops grown in nature simply by nature doing what nature does, pollinate, because they, Monsanto, patented a genetically modified seed. What then can people do in order to eat if not go to the corporation and pay if they can no longer get in nature what once was free, what once was their natural right?

The corporate race is making the human race dependent upon it instead of nature and again, this is to the detriment of humanity. Technology is aiding the corporation in this instance while at the same time devastating the environment it finds itself in. No longer do people see worms in their apples or corn, onions no longer make people tear, and the honey bee is dying off. To this, corporations like Sygenta and Monsanto are holding "Bee Summits" and opening research centers[51] into the disappearing honey bee. They are merely surrounding the problem with capital and dispersing currency to prove effort, when it is they that are the cause and the problem. The

---

[51] Reference Section II

"I" are the humans who gain, rising downward, from the profits of the corporate race, Lex Luther's to General Zod, but who then is the Ubermensch? Who then is the Confucian ghost of Plato's philosopher king?

The corporate race drains the human race's environment of its resources increasing the dependency of humanity on technology which has become a liability and no longer an advantage. So socialization between the human and corporate race occurs simultaneously with human to human socialization. The "I" mastered the art of this corporation to human socialization while the "We", for the most part are content with the crumbs from the master's table.

As previously stated, only in the face of that great enemy terrorism do the "I" and "We" become one. But even the act of terrorism proves how the government king insures the corporate race's survival. After 9/11 all financial institutes were shut down. A human could not get their own money from an ATM. The government effectively, learning from the market crash of 1929, kept the one thing that keeps the system tied together, its capital. Holding everyone's money captive until the terror became less frightening insured that the human race, in their moment of fear, would not leave the corporate race to die. Coincidentally the ATM replaced the need for excess tellers (jobs for humans) in banks, insuring a greater profit for banks, who in turn placed ATM fees on a thing that was supposed to be more efficient and cheaper than actual human workers. The "I" replace the "We" with machines in order to increase profits and the efficiency of the corporate race, never realizing that after all the "We" have been replaced by technology only the "I" will be left to be replaced.

Advancement's in technology have also made humanity despise time. They have made humans self-oriented, self-concerned, about me, be yourself by promoting yourself. Why wait in line at the supermarket while some human miscounts your money or can barely scan your items faster than you? Why write a novel and try to find an agent who then tries to sell it to a publishing house that then must market your novel and put it on the shelves of stores when you can do it yourself? That hard to find album a friend told you about, why ask them for the name then go from music store to music store conversing with strangers about a common interest, music, driving from town to town to each store meeting countless people along the way, seeing different sights, eating different foods all for a cd when you can click a button and buy it online. Why ask another person a question when you can just Google it? And lastly, why talk face to face with people when you can text, smh, lol, and hash tag your thoughts behind a persona on a social network, presenting an image of one's self before actually presenting the physical of one's self to the other persona's on social networks who do the same?

All the aforementioned are done for convenience, but *the loss of freedom begins with the want of convenience.* The more convenience an empire gets/gives, the less freedom its citizens have, the closer that empire is to being ravaged by its own advancements. Humans are the corporation. Humans are the government. Humans are the humans. The "I" willingly sacrifice themselves' for the perceived greater good in hopes of first, benefiting themselves, and sixtiethly, benefit the "We". Partaking in the social contract, better yet they write the social contract in order to take the natural power of those who do not realize they are more than Esaus and then begin socialization. The "We" are then sacrificed as well by the "I", whether willing or unwilling, the "We" will partake in the social contract.

Generation after generation from century to century the human population continues increasing and with it, the price of consumable goods. The price a consumer pays for these goods must reflect the true cost of production, but as previously stated this reflection is not true. Herein lies the reason why all throughout history, all prior empires have been novice. All novice empires come into existence for convenience. It is more convenient to use currency in exchange for services than to be the farmer, the mechanic, the architect, the warrior, the leader, the artist, the teacher etc. all embodied in one human. The currency represents the government under which these services are rendered. Allowing the mechanic to purchase the goods the farmer sells as well as allowing the farmer to buy the services the mechanic provides at an alleged fair exchange outside of equivalent labor for equivalent labor, which would be more time consuming, less convenient. But since all empires have been novice, they all use this extra step, this currency, this capital as a fair exchange. It is not an exchange of equivalence. In fact, *humanity is a paycheck away from being homeless. The rails steers the train*, but in order to cease the building of novice empires, humanity, as a whole, must understand how to lay the tracks, for the

rails have always been.

VII

In recent years, time has seemed to accelerate, that is to say, how we experience time has changed. This is in part due to our technology evolving at an exponential rate, not just doubling, but doing so in Fibonacci fashion. The more advanced our technology gets, the smaller the world in which we live in becomes. So goes the same for communication. The greater the speed of communication, the less aware of time one is, almost to the point that time is lost in the experience. To assuage this, we are entertained. In a phrase, time becomes a byproduct of experience. Experience then is a structured design created by a system intended on reducing experience from being unique to the individual to a banal exercise worked out by the masses in society. It benefits that which gives the structured design to fabricate unity through shared experience and not through a shared cause, as a cause, righteous or not, becomes an imminent threat to that which gave the structured design.

What is being said is that our time is being taken and in its place experience is exchanged. But even our memories of experiences are limited, "Even the very best photographs do not represent reality; they result from an act of selection and impose a limit on something that has none." Though first published in 1956, these words are as applicable to social media as they were to the photograph because they are both the resulting views of the partaker having the experience, and what they chose to capture for their own memory or for the memory of the technology used to capture their experience, in route to sharing it with the rest of society.

The structured design comes into play for example, when a child goes to Cape Canaveral visiting the Kennedy Space Center for the first time and gets a cup of space dots/dippin dots while there. When this child becomes an adult they watch the movie Another Earth where one character asks her other-self from the other Earth to write down what she had at Kennedy Space Center and she responds space dots/dippin dots. The same thing her other-self had, the same thing the viewer of the movie had there as a child.

The point of this is to illustrate how what was supposed to be a unique experience becomes a banal exercise. The government king owns the Kennedy Space Center while one corporation prince owns the space dots/dippin dots and another corporation prince owns the studio where the movie was made, all partaking in the fabrication of a human memory while reducing the experience to a banal exercise. So the adult whose experience as a child felt unique to them is actually a structured design experienced by the masses in society.

The child actually experienced it and the character in the movie experienced it as well the adult viewer vicariously re-experiencing it through the character as they view the movie. The corporate race provided the structured design for the child to experience it in reality. The corporate race provided the structured design for the movie that allowed the character to share the same experience that the adult viewer had as a child, still, in the movie, the corporate race owned the Kennedy Space Center. So the experience, now a banal exercise, no longer unique to the individual, but shared by the masses in society, is a structured design fabricated by the corporate race mimicking the human race through a system meant to replace that which is done naturally[52].

If the corporate race can create and control the experiences humans have, then the time spent having these experiences falls under the ownership of the corporation, which in turn selects what experiences are at the forefront of society's memory and through what medium the memories will be triggered. Through entertainment, time becomes the byproduct of experience. Memories, though not all, are now created by the corporate race and shared by them and the human race alike, the former using these memories to increase profits while the latter feebly still believe that these are precious memories of natural experiences created by themselves when they are actually banal exercises orchestrated by the corporate race to increase profits. An unwitting deigning occurs as memories become "an act of selection" by the corporate race, imposing limits on something that has none, in this case time and memory of human beings.

---

[52] Reference Section VI

Now the world decreases in size as technology advances, and time, increasingly becoming a byproduct of experience, becomes less important, to the point that the saying, "where did the time go" means nothing. A transition takes place from what and how you remember an experience being the natural responsibility of the human being to becoming the incessant want of the corporation, who constantly insists, through all forms of social media that humans depend on to keep their memories forever present shared with all online. This want stems from the need of profits and how to achieve a way of making all things profitable.

Instant connection in regard to communication hastens yet another more important transition and that being the one where experience goes from being a byproduct of time to time becoming a byproduct of experience. Experiences that become banal and the same for the whole of humanity, communicated in an instant, done in little to no time, reduces the necessity of one being aware of time. All this is done with the hopes of suppressing/eventually eliminating original thought. For the lack of original thought disqualifies a society from challenging the governing thought, ultimately penning every human signature to the social contract. "Each man must be stripped of his own powers, and given powers which are external to him, and which he cannot use without the help of others."

In this case, that power being stripped is the power of original thought and the external power being giving is the collective memory of an experience that is nothing more than a banal exercise orchestrated by the corporation prince to increase profits. As technology advances, the importance of time is slowly minimized and the importance of experience is maximized. Time, being intrinsic to humans, as it is the chosen denomination that marks our lineal physiological progression from birth to death as well as our historical progression, must be minimized so that we can become depended solely on technology to denote our lineal physiological and historical progression. In this way, technology, a thing imbued within the corporation, aids the corporate race in making the human race predictable, our behavior tailored and less threatening to it.

The human race, having entered a state of indentured servitude with the corporate race, no longer has to "remember the time"; we must only click a button and show the perspective of which the experience was captured to whomever we want to share the experience/banal exercise with. Time becomes a byproduct at this point because experiences now occur and are shared simultaneously, so time is not needed to denote when the experience occurred because the whole of society experienced it in some form of medium at the same time via technology. Thus the experience becomes forever present i.e. panoramic, as each human captures the experience from a different perspective/angle recreating the experience in its entirety, in essence making that experience forever present leaving time as a mere byproduct of the experience.

Humanity, now falling from its state of divine monarchy, swindled out of its natural powers by its own creations, the government king and the corporation prince, willingly enter this state of indentured servitude simply for the want of convenience, signing this new *corporate social contract*, relinquishing our natural freedom. As unique experiences are exchanged for the banal exercises, the original thought that so often stems from unique experiences disappears and in its place the same redundant thoughts and ideas shared by all who now share these fabricated banal exercises created by the corporation prince. These shared experiences/banal exercises are less of a threat to the government king and corporation prince than a shared cause or ideal because it was a shared ideal and cause that created the corporate race to begin with. It is imperative at this point to restate that the seeds of a novice empire's destruction are sewed at its inception. Aware of this paradox, the corporate race attempts to eliminate that which can destroy it, the same way it does by first shutting down all the banks immediately after an act of terrorism. With the human race seemingly defeated, the corporate race has no choice but to fight amongst itself.

So how does a creation of the human race fight amongst itself? What weapons are used? It is not that the corporate race fights itself, no; it is more like the corporation prince usurping the crown from its parent the government king. This regicide of sorts is accomplished by starving the government king, by not feeding it the profits it needs to survive. The corporation prince is now at the point where it has begun to experiment with alternative currency, it is on the verge of completely severing its capital ties to the government king.

It too has a social contract. It too has "made Artificiall Chains" for itself and must return to the yoke it so desperately attempts to throw off its back. As Adam was the divine monarch under God, and humans male and female had dominion over everything under Adam, and everything under the humans male and female were subjected to all of the aforementioned, so has the human race become to the corporation prince who is subjected to the human monarch the government king, who began as servant to the human race.

But we are ahead of ourselves. Returning to this idea of alternative currency, it will in effect isolate the government king, ultimately giving those who sought smaller government, privatization etc. what they have always wanted, the end of government, the death of the government king. In all cases the created has become greater than the creator. The human race creates the corporate race and eventually falls victim to the same. The government king births the corporation prince and is eventually starved out, falling victim to that which it birthed. The human race ravages the environment in which it lives, believing that it is insuring its survival when it is actually accomplishing the opposite. The corporate race ravages the human race, the environment by which it exists, believing it is insuring its survival, when it too is actually insuring its very own demise. In a word or three, the collective human mind is schizophrenic, sociopathic, self-destructive, and these attributes are reflected in the corporate race. In a phrase, *the rails steers the train*. Humanity must not be afraid to stop the train, adjust the direction of the rails, and lay new tracks.

Works Cited

CCA. (2012). Retrieved from Correctional Corporation of America:
  http://www.cca.com/about/

drug library. (2012). Retrieved from
  http://www.druglibrary.org/prohibitionresults.htm

NYPD. (2013, May 22). Retrieved from NYPDrecruit:
  http://www.nypdrecruit.com/exam-center/exam-overview

Baudrillard, J. (1994). *Simulacra and Simulation.* The Univeristy of
  Michigan Press.

Camus, A. (1956). *The Rebel.* New York: Vintage Books.

Hayek, F. (2007). *The Road to Serfdom Text and Documents The Definitve
  Edition.* Chicago: The University of Chicago Press.

Hobbes, T. (2004). *Leviathan.* Barnes & Noble Publishing, Inc.

Locke, J. (2012). *Two Treatises of Government.* New York: Cambridge
  University Press.

Machiavelli, N. (1970). *The Discourses on the First Decade of Titus Livy.*
  London: Penguin.

Nietzsche, F. (2005). *Thus Spoke Zarathustra.* New York city: Barnes &
  Nobles Classics.

Payne, T. (1986). *Common Sense.* London: Penguin Books.

Rand, A. (1957). *Atlas Shrugged.* New York : Plume.

Rousseau, J.-J. (1968). *The Social Contract.* London: Penguin Books.

Singer, A. (2012, February 27). *About Us: Citizens for tax justice is 501 (c)(4) research group and advocacy organization focused on federal, state, and local tax policies*. Retrieved from Citizens for tax justice: http://www.ctj.org/taxjusticedigest/archive/2012/02/press_release_general_electric.php

Witt, J. (2009). *SOC.* New York: McGraw-Hill.

Email questions or comments about On the Novice Empire to

flackl@live.com

www.ingramcontent.com/pod-product-compliance
Lightning Source LLC
Chambersburg PA
CBHW051811040426
42446CB00007B/621